PARABLES OF THE BIBLE

PARABLES OF THE BIBLE

The House on the Rock

Drejervej 15,3 DK-2400 Copenhagen NV, Denmark
Tel.: (+45) 3531 0330 Fax: (+45) 3531 0334
E-mail: info@scanpublishing.dk
Website: www.scanpublishing.dk

Design by Ben Alex
Printed in China
ISBN 87 7247 781 4 (Hard cover)
ISBN 87 7247 777 6 (Soft cover)

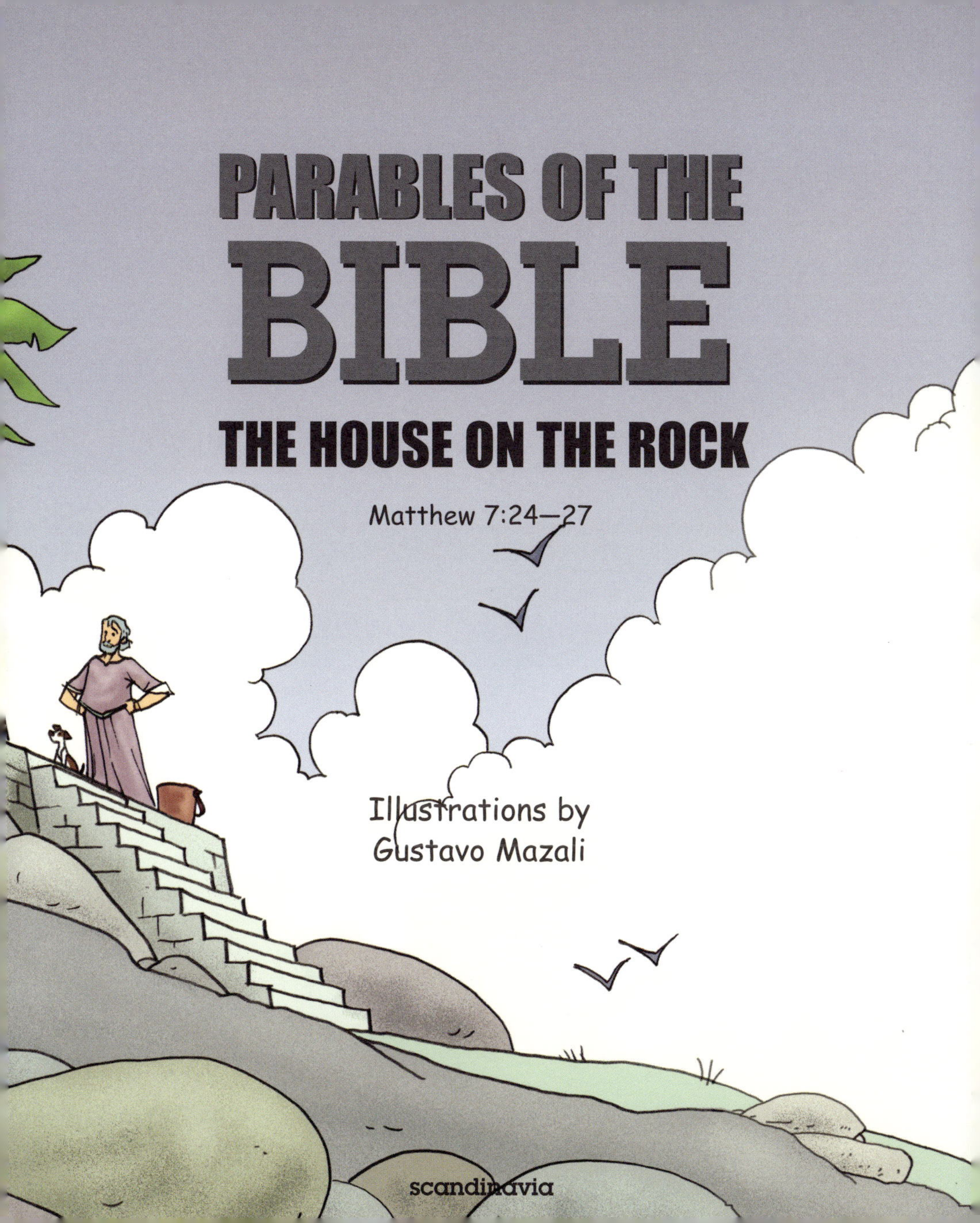

PARABLES OF THE BIBLE

THE HOUSE ON THE ROCK

Matthew 7:24—27

Illustrations by
Gustavo Mazali

scandinavia

Two friends

There once were two friends who were thinking about building their own homes. They talked about it and looked for places to build. Finally each of them decided where he would build his home. Then they began to haul in building materials.

The foolish man

The first man wanted a home with a beautiful view. So he began building his house on the beach. He didn't even think about that he was building his house on sand. This was foolish because sand is no foundation for a house.

The foolish man wouldn't listen

The other man was wiser. He went over to his foolish friend and told him it's a bad idea to build a house on sand. But the foolish friend wouldn't listen.

"I like it here," he said. "See the beautiful view!"

The wise man's house

The wise man found a flat area away from the beach.

"This is where I will build my house," he said, "right here on this sturdy rock." He knew this was a safe place to build his house.

A terrible storm

One night there came a terrible storm. The foolish man was frightened and ran outside—just in time to save his life. Soon the wind crushed the house, and the waves washed it into the sea.

Standing strong

Meanwhile, the wise man sat safely in his house that was built on the sturdy rock. Although the wind blew and blew, the house stood strong. The wise man was not afraid. He knew he had built his house on firm ground.

The house on the rock

—read the story in the Bible

"Therefore everyone who hears these words of mine and puts them into practice is like a wise man who built his house on the rock. The rain came down, the streams rose, and the winds blew and beat against that house; yet it did not fall, because it had its foundation on the rock. But everyone who hears these words of mine and does not put them into practice is like a foolish man who built his house on sand. The rain came down, the streams rose, and the winds blew and beat against that house, and it fell with a great crash."

Matthew 7:24-27